POMPOUS HANG GLIDER TALK

what is your business here
with that gear
slung over the racks
on the roof of your horseless car?
where are you going with your molten rose
beside you with her orange scarf, where this
summer
do you go with that mummified canoe
stretched on the rack of your automobile
making terminable lines of motorists
burn in the squirm of the cat's disease
to know what creature the bright cocoon
conceals?
what high hill at the beaches,
where are the current skeins of the airs
do you wish to be caught consorting
with
you aerial minstrels in moods fey and aeolian

you do not hesitate to escape the fouled fisherman's
birdsnest

you crave the escape from the fouled fisherman's
birds nest
that every man has looked on with despair
(in an oily parka in the rain on kelpy rocks)

you don't hesitate to escape the pursuit
of this glum contemplation
the tangled threatening skein
that runs through each man's brain

My only purpose has been
to serve the Muse,
reveal art and ~~study~~
archetype.   present

TABLE OF CONTENTS

FOREWORD

As long as we can remember, Dad wrote. Passion is a word sometimes overused, but in this case, it is fitting for Dad - he had a passion for both the written and spoken word; he was a wordsmith, a word lover, a word philosophiser. He loved the origin of words and the history steeped in their stories. He loved the sound of words whispered to the wind or bellowed to the farthest mountain. Last but not least, of course, he was a storyteller. A painter and sculptor of words; he gave words life and spread joy and wonder, with words.

When Ceridwyn was with Dad in September 2018, the month he died, he said to her, "Do you remember me writing lots when you were a child?" She nodded and said she had vivid memories of him typing intently, madly typing with one finger, whereupon he turned away dreamily and said ***"All I have ever done is follow the muse. When I was younger, I wrote more. Then I was busy telling. These last months I have been writing again. But I have always just followed the muse..."***

We all hope to feel we have mattered in this world, that we have left a lingering mark. Dad wanted to leave his words, he wanted to publish his creative works. Sadly he wasn't afforded enough time to make that dream a reality.

Dad: this book, a sample of the huge body of creative work you left behind, is part of your legacy; the rest lies within the hearts of all who knew you. In those hearts you will never be forgotten.

To Beth who began this project for Dad, many thanks. To Linus, one of Dad's dear friends, overwhelming thanks are due. The three of us daughters have been so exhausted by life, work and grief in the last year that without Linus' energy and hours and hours of transcribing, this book would not have been finished, not for a much longer time anyway. To Dad: we miss you terribly but rest assured that you, and your words, stay with us always.

Corrina, Ceridwyn & Natasha

EXPLORING THE *Myth*

WE IN THE WILD WIND WENT

In the wild wind we went,
drawn, earth sick maenads
drunk on ecstasy
into the Pan-maddened trees
into the drenched grass
rampant vines, tawny and bold,
Better than a heather bed,
The canopy of leaf-weave branches
Swan high above
Like mad heads of lover's hair
With soft violence moved by the winds of desire,
and we threw ourselves down,
our bodies were enwrapt and hot, strong:
we in the wild wind went,
The ecstasy of Dionysus
hammering in our blood
shaking us and the earth and gasping trees
We left the earth awe earthlorn love strong
maenads,
Screaming in the lust and the happy power,
Shrieking in the scream of the winds
impassioned like the gods amidst creation
entwined in the navel whorl of the world,
in the centre of the she-earth entangled
drunk in rapture in the Pan-stepped wood
in the wild wind we went

we wrong in the wild wind
to the love-swept swoly of the whorl of the world
loving in the sinews rampant of the viney
grass,
tawny and bold,
Better than a heather bed.

March 25th 1991
From the wildness.

APRIL FOOLS' DAY 1967

Cobbles on a struck street paved stone clattering
Small stones loud feet deep wet pools.
Horse no rider tries galloping galloping:
But the inn-keeper's monkey just calls and calls.

High walls no tops dearth of air chokes the sky
Lay eggs brush flies plant your lap of seed.
Three clowns glee laugh jump high high:
Ape joins organ-grinder for his daily feed.

Boys make bird-pie now the roofs are naked
Glut faces steal apples from the ragtail cripple.
Clean hands black hands clowns arms akimbo
Struck stones cry out masked faces claw a nipple.

A BLIND CHINAMAN AND HIS WIFE

In this man who moved in front of me
Were two dead eye-balls, his sight
A small woman of China, to see
His way out of large night.

She had her hands tight about his arm
And when she saw me, young of a day life
She stopped the man, moving her fingers of
relinquished charm
Onto the worn grey tie about his neck O wife

of a blind man,
have the alien movements of you both,
and your old stretched skin, made your eyes loathe
the glances of other people?
Where are your childhood people,

And have you in these times sighed
For the return of the days when your lord had sight,
When it was his strength and his eyes
That made you say, Life is not lies?

1965

BY THE LONG GATE
THE RIPE CLAY COMES

The mother standing by the long gate
Is waiting for the tall son to come
    Though he is high and waving in the sun
    Between child and man she will dilate.
She must stay awhile in this heated land.

The middle times when she washed his wounds
Have lain away almost ten years now:
Her hands would bless, but they know not how:
    The clay was made hard by ten huge noons.
She must stay awhile in this heated land.

Had her life been wound betwixt her man
She might have made her spouse her home
    And lived in joy, as the pope in Rome
    But the house was out of joint no plan.
She must stay awhile in this heated land.

So turned her eye round to her bold son
And told him the right and wrong of life
And burnt herself on his envisioned pyre
                Beat the drums, blow the fife!
So down to the long gate she'll come.

She must go away from this place,
From more damage in this heated land.

1966 

THE BLACK FOX AT MY SIDE

The Black Fox at my side, he always said
    The apple-blossom is pink but its days short:
So let the wind scatter petals the sky sought
    Do not leave them on the branches dead.

I laid my hand in his teeth, and in his ears
    I told him of the dazzled night lights
And the hands moving and the eye-whites –
    Yet he pointed at dried tears.

This Black Fox, he always laughed at my notions:
    When the wind is fair, then blossoms must fly
And the jealous winds, they may vie
    For the pink of the petal with its potions

yet the blossoms go, and the winds circle
    in their mournful dirge of a lost light:
Maybe a petal will come and stay tight
    In the eddies of a joyful wind, and circle

to tie its ebb and rot and fly apart in the eddies of
this joyful wind.
    This Black Fox at my side, his teeth
They come to a smile from a snarl and a dark wreath
    of skin curls ugly round the sinned

gleam of his dancing eyes –
    I tug at the folds of skin behind his neck
    I kiss his old white teeth and the foam-flack
And set about telling my lies.

CARNIVAL OF THE MOON

The moon is wandering,
I am wakeful, I do not sleep,
I stare at the night and think of mountain tracks,
For I know the moon is lingering over fallen
stones of Greece,
roving over rooves of Argos and of Nafplion,
a squashed disc magnified low in the sky,
brushing brief golden sparkles through stone
manes of shaggy lions carven over the Lion Gate.

Splashing amber over Umbrian clay.

I fling open the windows
barefoot I step out onto warm clay tiles,
like a tai chi master I move,
in the form of a slow daddy-long-legs
though my shoeless feet were like new foal's hooves
delicately picking at the pathways of the rooves –
moonlight covers me as I walk the terracotta
Leaning on a chimney-pot I whisper Te adoro
to the basilica lacquered with platinum light
I cannot scry any transcendent meaning anywhere,
unless holding one another holds meaning.

Let's try holding one another then,
hold me, hold me
let me read the inscriptions in your eyes

let me feel the long satin stroke of your look,
is it fondly retaining significant moments?

Upon the altar of change we sacrifice the constant.
There is no goddess more hungry than the moon.

If the moon makes me dance on Grecian rooves
it is making someone dance in Buenos Aires,
it makes everyone a ghost on the slippery slopes
of Wellington,
and if the moon is lighting up Bohemian Puhoi
and gold-sifted Lawrence,
if it is lighting up the contested stones of Athens,
its streets, its windows, its doorways,
then it will light narrow houses up from the Basin
Reserve –

I have walked down those streets in winter nights,
the houses still, asleep and brittle, crystalline –

I with memories of going around in the moonlight,
standing staring at the Caledonian Hotel,
the last drunkard tottering to a room down
Tasman Street,
me sitting on frost silvered steps,
talking to weird intense girls
with high cheekbones

about folk music and psychics,
weird intense girls I longed to kiss,
who blew me kisses at the letterbox,
while their real kisses fell on the lips
of someone who wasn't me.

Windows slivered with patterned ice
Frost crackled down from the distant sky
until dawn
the stars have long since rusted away
into the night of another world
leaving behind only the ping of starry shards
God it was cold walking her home
past Basin Reserve,
the Swiss refugee from the camps
standing out of the lamp-light
his tattooed arm and his wine,
we're walking through the cold cold night.
and I wish she'd turn and put her warm mouth on
my aching lips,
can all your kisses be spoken for elsewhere?

The sister of the sun remains
But no-one quite sees the real stars anymore,
the sky is so vast, it's easy to feel forgotten,
when just then I see a flash of light
at an attic window,
moonlight in the eyes, a woman has caught fire,
she leans out, stargazing,
her moonriven eyes shine through raven hair,

what's she sighing for?

the unforgiving moon sends her aluminium fluid
oozing over the rooftops,
sloshing over the furniture
in post-midnight rooms
leaking under doorways
in the shapes of wet ghosts.

As you walk vaguely homewards
over husks of bygone streams in dusky hollows
lace brushed with lunar silver in the low woods,
you make your legs navigate unfamiliar geometries
you're frightened, it's a maze of angled alleys
you stumble along obscure and unmarked lanes
night has changed to purple and your feet are
going lame

shaking like a half-finished animation,
stalking dissociated phantoms in Prague
making your way on sloping diagonals in a park,
shade spilling around the corner like squid's ink
your shadow is projected on high-windowed walls
by that hungry goddess with an appetite
for the absolute
of alteration and alternative.

A dark doorway swings open, I shuffle up,
tottering on the cobbles, I look within
I catch you shivering
in the moonlit filmset of Shackleton's hut

I pick up discarded film
from the floor beneath my feet
I see your fleeting figure
but moonshine has overexposed you.

I feel the reeling sun burning on my neck,
l hear the laugh you gave on summer days
I turned my head,
I thought I'd see you swiping balls
along the bright shores of tennis on the lawn
creamily lit by pleats swishing from the hips of
shouting girls,

but you have stepped back
into medieval oaks and elms
in long patches at the edge or the court's end,
light-parched, the moon does not visit that far,
a sward of deep shade like a dark hawk swoops

something has swallowed you

I heard a shutting sound
I looked away, I didn't see,
maybe you stepped through
some softly-thudding door
into a scratched film dream
where faint waterlogged images shove past,
dragging drunkenly through foggy streets
like soldiers trying to save each other in the
smokescreens,
calling for help, unheard and blinded

For in spite of love,
mountains or love, oceans of love,
forests gorged with lover's trysts,
rising passions, earth-enfolding love,
wolves and geese plighting their troth for life,
man and women standing making love in
midsummer streams,
everyone in one another's arms, tender words and
loving eyes,

in spite of all this loving,
few escape suffering,
The wounded and lost lurch past me,
words drily whisper through throats hoarse
from hailing the dead
they stagger past lampposts with broken bulbs
they search the pavements, they search
stairwells,
they call out the names of everyone they knew,
they call out the names of their bedmates,
whom they climbed into sleep with,
night after night, for years,
snuggling into her or him,
nuzzling warm, burning in places
arms winding round bodies like hot plasticine.

I hear them speaking into the night, resting,
hands holding vines by an overgrown fence,

'Give me the balm of a warm bed in winter,

Lying close to him.
Lying close to her.

Feeling her scented hair straying over my face
As she slept and l lay awake,
and her warm cheek on mine, and her soft breath
like the slow stirring of a feather falling past my lips,
as I sunk again into sleep.'

'Give me the peace of body curled in his

He curled around me his chest and belly warmed
my back,
as I lay when I was a child in my mother's womb,
lying curled and dreaming in the warm sea of
incipience,
and he holding my breasts tenderly,
nipples pressed to the centre of his palms,
the front of his thighs on the back of my thighs
his shins on my calves
his toes slowly stroking my feet, tops and soles.'

I float like an angel flying above me.
I look down - there she is, there he is,
curling together as you have heard,

I look down from the riffle of my angel wings,
I see below me limbs move and a face looks up,
for a moment I saw the memory of our rapturous selves
held in that now that was then,

Yet I remember watching you,

in the luminescence of the stars
my moon-frosted eyelashes trembling,

I looked at you from the French doors,
while you dipped black pastels into wet moons
made by tears which you upon your palette shed,
dark smudges smeared the sketch-pad of your sorrow
shaking pastels across the paper bled and bled.

Then you took in hand charcoal from burnt-out wood,
you became an artist of the noir,
How much black do you let the daytime have?
How much dark can you take out of the night'?

'Come love, let's give ourselves up again to close
embrace
When we found each other in one another's arms
halfway to the dawn, a thirdway woken,
but not awake, still sleeping but not asleep,
her head against my throat
my arms all around her, his arms around me,
her warm skin feeling as if her skin was growing
inside mine
and my skin was growing inside his
my veins your veins, my breath your breath.

We poetised about ourselves
as two of the seven seas,
whose urge to merge had made them quite heroic,'

'Seas between us broad did roar,

We surged through currents sear
as cold as when the Snow Queen pees
she surely made us freeze,
parts of us were stepping-stones
for paws of polar bears,
when one day rose a bright new moon,
it rose above a berg of ice
lying like the crown of Isis on the peak,
and we were on opposite shores of the ice,
But I was rolling in from the north-east,
you couldn't see me
you were lapping in from the harsh south-west,
I couldn't see you.

but as we got closer we began to steam
From the Age of Fire we came,
from beneath the sea we boiled
with the wet heat at thermal streams
coming together with guttural screams,
we shot jets of scalding brine up to the stars
we were the hottest of the seven seas
when we at last met, we melted continents of ice
wc couldn't help that, we were molten ourselves

After sunrise,
different parts of us were still meeting
our limbs kept behaving like the currents of the sea
my knee flowing in the hair where her legs begin,
she muzzling towards me there, tenderly

We spoke poetry to each other lying there nuzzling,
we spoke epic love drama, we made up love letters,
words sprang up, though I don't remember
composing them
it was the love muse making our lips say
what should not be regretted or forgotten.

Time was not invented then,
though there was infinite space tor holding,

Oh angel, bring us back to that cosy place
where we spoke thus, and held thus,
make a time when we can hold, and speak, and hold!'

These words I hear the seas of lost souls call,
trying to speak out through thirsty throats,
lips cracked,
while all around they hear the mocking ones
All good, is it? Sweet as? – Did you say sweet?'

There's a woman you recognise,
you stare but she won't meet your eyes,
she turns and hurries down the street
you follow through crowded arcades
you're stumbling through the phantom shades
but the face you seek most eludes and evades.

If I found you I'd put the billy on for a brew,
drinking endless sweet tea as I did once with you,
when we watched a full moon eclipse into blood,
it hung like an orange, my hand opened –

our skins were drenched with darkroom red,
I remember your emerald eyes were crimson edged
while honeyed green tea ran out of our ears,
our hearts deluded by the music of the spheres.

You flung your arms up, you called to the stars,
Give me paints and canvas from the cosmos,
Give me a brush to just dash off a night like this!
It's only rocks in random space,
but look at what the moon can do with light!

Earth shifted, colours changed, eclipse passed,
Moon in daytime form arose with dawn,
her watching face was pale, like yours,
washed-out and drawn
in shadow masked
a carven map of crossroads you have known,

lightly rubbing the lines beneath your eyes,
you gave away your craving for immorality
which even your subtle glance could not disguise.

desiring again that time before the rising of the sun
when we lay speaking ancient words of love
when 'bliss' was the only word my mind would think,
when 'love, love' were the only sounds my lips
would make
that time when everything in our room became
golden,

splurging juicily from a moon rising fat and huge,
spilling over the world's edge covering us with
artist's gilt
and we felt like Danae,
the gods and goddesses were making love to us,
we were transmuted,
you went to the open window and sang,
sea-salty air blew gold-dust over our unclad skins
the sun melted gold over the rooftops,
It was a long journey the moon did with us that night,

but skin to skin we gladly held our warmly woken
bodies
we laughed, it was a twenty-four carat morning.

HARROWED TRIBES

The birdling's guttering has rusted and fallen
    The nests are broken.
Straws are turning in the gathering mud
    And the house is in flood.

The eggs have time ago risen and flown
    The breath has grown;
Waters sift the shells in the whispering grass
    The cry of these sparrows is past.

Bread is cast at the shores of the lake,
    And the ducks awake.
No hand will break down this home and their birth
– Still waters are the earth.

The harrowed tribes are searching for their hearth
    In an unflared path.
There is no ball or hole or stump or stone
    Or blood or bone
    That is their own.

May 1967

UNTITLED

I was there the day when they
Anathematized the flowers –
When Aton at Heliopolis
Disclaimed his title to the Sun,
when chairmen, presidents and primes
placed placentas in their wines.

We were present at the side
of many a tickering android bride
who within a year had died
of boredom for she could not find
a leaf to decorate her mate
for leaves were in pretty short supply
after the spray they thought might kill the fly
and her programmer was myopic with
Swiss watch slung across his coat
from an eighteenth-century house of fame,
and the botanical nodes of his programming
were really rather out of date.

Oh I looked on when the android brides
conferred while standing by the sea
about the humanoids they'd seen;
and the sea was beautifully clear that day
and the brides bubbling to the surface
laughed and said that underneath they

could see for miles and miles;
and then their memory nodes released
according to prescribed and regulated intervals
a tear.
the sea was awfully clear that day
the plankton all had gone away
(and will not come again another day).

And we stood respectfully by the day
nodes anaesthetized the brides
when humanoid contact stops, he said,
nodding and twinkling in his spectacles
wondering about his next fishing holiday,
'You shall after a little while
Lie down, good child, and sleep.'

We watched, while they slept:
for we had been present when
they anathematised the flowers
when Ra sucked in his commanding
                life-force of the Sun
when men of (tailored) quality and of
                some kind of philanthropy
place placentas in their wines
and spat into the seas.

RE**INVENT**ING EVERYDAY **LIFE**

ROOM PEOPLE

Weighty thoughts oppress me, and I take
Pink tea drinkers to hell with me
They can smirk - they drink weak tea, nod seriously,
Agree, and daintily rebut conversant
Theorise, and criticise with no intent
No intent, no purpose, than to prove they are they
The fools of the drawing room
All stiffened in slinking cloth, who play music
And breathe.

THE MINE OF THE INTROSPECTIVE MAN

Mine is the introspective man
driving home to a chip
bar in the centre of a flower
from the living desert

the desert with flowers in silent doom
blooming through untimed centuries,
no one is going to use a stop-watch
here

unmined is the introspective man
who stands tentatively by the flood-gates
fingering the Kodachrome memories
in his wallet

until a supervisor shouts:

The introspective man who is mine
turns, his lips filled with shame,
not able to share the pain
of the loss of his wallflowers again,
mute as clams
while the floodgates of dams
open like his mouth when it says I am

when it can,
as unwatered orchids dawn
when they can

mine is the lost
consciousness
floating like golden Egyptians
quietly drowning under the Red Sea.

The watch has stopped.
Tentative and introspective,
keeping his thoughts to himself,
he strolls back to town

fingering the negatives
of his coloured memories

in the deep eye of his mind

INSENSIBLE RULES

It is better not to proceed without some grand
ground-rules
– remember the ground nuts that became so well
defined?

rules are crushing: that is why we call them ground,
like coffee-beans, so they may be all
the more easily
assimilated
NOT because we want our rules
to be rooted in the good earth
– we would not call them ground rules then –

People who enjoy ground rules
should be shut up in Kafka's Castle
writing guidelines for intercommunications
between ant and aphid –
there's a protocol there too –

as for letting the rule makers off,
that's rash:
let them think they have entered paradise,
while we experiment with chaos
lighting our bonfires
with the rules
that so cleverly confound
the loftiest aspirations. 

THE GIRL WHO GOT OUT OF
THE SANDWICH SHOP

The girl in the sandwich
    shop
        sighs
and rustling to the tables
            in her nylon dress
thinks of Joan Baez
the mountains of love and protest
drip like petals from the wind
    into her waterfalling mind
that roars at her all day

while her mystic eyes
can make no sense
of unsprung rolls or custard tarts

There is a woman in the corner swollen with mortality
(who used to feign youth until her dermatitis and
senility
devoured her
and on her lavatory wall
she has copied in a steady calligraphy
'beauty is but a flower')

she starts wearing her heart on her sleeve
for the girl in the brittle nylon,

the girl who plucks petals from the currents of her
sorrows
and reads them,
    interpreting,
passing them silkenly
                over her moving lips,

– The lady who once feigned youth
has opened her mouth in gluttony
revealing a depravity of cavities,

she begins to tell the toy faced girl

how her first husband wouldn't give her a thing
and her second like that too
and the days of her life spill out
like the segments of a tapeworm
enticed from his parasitical suppertime
                                into the light

 The mystic eyes of the toy faced nylon girl expand
(behind the scenes she sits on a green bank by a
jacaranda
taking profusions of petals
                to examine)

Listen, dear, says the old duck
take my advice and don't let them –

(the waterfall is Niagarating
in the navigational unfix of her brain:
the songs of love and protest
that she understood too well
are playing the Olympian Furies
at 2000 watts or more –
the bank shores up no longer and subsides
into the dark death of speculation)

She sits now under the real jacaranda tree
real petals in her lap

(The bloated female spider
squats still in her corner daily
wincing at her soft mortal decay
blurting her life's agony
                    at the walking frescoes
who are obliged to serve her.)

BUNCH OF FLOWERS

A lady stood at the roadside afar off
she held what seemed to me a bunch of flowers
so fervently clasped, and the waiting,
the waiting so vibrant in her stance
that I believed she waited for her lover.

Then she folded up her newspaper
which she could not do to a bunch of flowers

a bus slid up to her soundlessly
she stepped in, and it carried her away.

I realised I was being romantic
again.
Then, again, I may not have been.

THE BLACK CAT STALKS THE HOUSE

The black cat walks over the blue hose
touching the nozzle with his nose
while a child, tying up its giggles,
turns on a tap.

But the black cat who has already
successfully
overcome the loops of the azure hose
recovers dignity

and moves casually aside
stalking the house,
stalking the house as its prey,
but the black cat makes a mistake
instead of clawing the house and carrying it away
he goes underneath, and prays
that the house will not claim him as its prey
but it does.

The Black Cat who minced finely
over the blue hose
treading
like on a carpet of marshmallow
has not been seen since
the house captivated him
In its dark underneath.

We think he is preparing some new feline assault:
he's done it before.

FIVE WATER-COLOURS

The spindly rhythm of a silly day
    winds and stops.
The leaves fall down no longer gay
    when the season drops.

In the park where the caretaker
    sweeps and sings
Leaves fall, leaves roll and their sound is heard
    when the wind sings.

When the rain-drops chatter on the window
    we look outside
And in their numbers on the concrete path
    worms die wide.

On a sandy beach in the big sun
    fish skulls glitter
Two white gulls in the dried day
    their hunger bitter.

The little girl fallen when guns come near
    guns from war
She had a new pinafore, the drums roll
    roll of drums.

THE WADING LANTERN

The wading lantern of my incoming tide
    (– Hola! hola! Says the white-patch clown)
Leaves the shoal no peace on the ship's right side
Give way! give way! For the nets to be drawn.

The flesh in the fire is browned well and eaten
(– Day three! day three! Smiles the sun in its heaven)
He spins his eyes to my gathering dawn
    Eat long! he calls, for the meat is warm.

Would the days that are wide had filled me brimfull
    (v Swing bladder! ring bells,
    grins the fool by my heel)
For I thirst while awaiting my severing pull –
    – Hold back! Tells my pulse, all turns on the wheel.

O the Rose in my earth is as long as the Song
    Can I not keep it?
Many days we have watered to bring forth the flower
    And our seed is golden.

First find the flesh of the fish in the fire
    Brown it and feed.
Live in the flames on the beach of your Sire
    Then let grow your seed.

22 April 1967

since cack-handled we bubbled Rotorua over the
gendering land
and sent post-cards to Europe of hot-pools and
glittering Maori boys
          with one
hand upon their cock-and-hoop but otherwise
stark not even a grass arse-covering hand-
twisted early native garment nevertheless
greenstone whirlygiguns bopping from
the lobes of the ears –

since royal happy we poi-poid and bagpiped
every stand of the Windsor House over
every school and sport-stadium of the north
and displayed in wreaths the imperial clans
at the foot of horse-rifled memorials in the south –

since we sent our fern-fluttering chin-jut
khaki beer-veined fag-lipped and
sun-stained fish-tripping ball-kicking leather-fed
blackberry-picking bandy son-of-guns and really
kind bastards
arse-over-kite into yet more stone memorials
and marble and brass –

since the real estate agent climbed the Tairua peninsula
that once seemed so like a woman's breast as you
drove to it out of the hill-mists that you
could stretch out fingers to touch its
erect peaks –
the locals told the picture with a grin,
and tickled the tits every year in a lumbering
and complicated homecoming race that few finished –
since the real estate agent skirted the slopes
and brought forth the yellow and blue warts
of a fourth-rate housing division on this peninsula
at Tairua –

since I have seen these things
my eyes have become old and brittle
and sunken into hollows

like black molten glass

in the gravel

at the crater bottom

of a quiet volcano

IN THE GARDEN

The diesel's twin horn signals the turn,
twice, briefly in the fernlight, the coffee time
the town lights, instructed, come suddenly –
and a jazz orchestra starts to distantly play

its first note unmistakably a twin horn.

we employ our sincere hydrangea-talk
we are no longer polio victims, gracias Mr Salk
the blue-white cauliflowers, subjects of our speech,
border our lawn
reminding me of aging aunts with rods of steel
instead of spines
moving against the refuge of the flowers-
                    cluckity-clack-

knowing so little of viticulture,
how shall I instruct these vines?
a drought is in the ground, the larch-tree rattles –
O dear I'm coming unstuck –
an antique bellows in my collected aunt whirrs
fanning a pristine furnace
the steel becomes soft, it bends, yet still terse:
now the lace-bark lady is able to be lost in lobelias
weeding the blue stars of her new universe
stowing her corruption into compost heaps
for re-cycling.

on the next day I watch the brown granite-man:
he strips off the netting from the pool, he stands
deep,
he repeatedly and finically dips his bucket,
seeking the one fish,
taking tangles out of the water
engaged in the removal of mischances
while the thirteenth-century nun in the sky
    lashes him with scalded brambles
until he beats the retreat inside to tea and scones.

up from the hill in the morning
come the dandelion seeds, propagating their species
floating in an orderly Handelesque mosaic
like the spirits of sea-eggs, transparent and shining
haunting the early world
the 5 a.m. gardeners possessed, looking:
an incense of rubbery smoke crawls
to the top of the sky
the slow ignition of new clippings
a recognition of waste

a girl smiles at the rotten peach between her toes
as indoors an oven upon a plucked goose
is closed, is closed
and a satisfied smile wafts from the kitchen window
over the khaki man on the grass lagoon
with the crackling scent of stuffing and roast
                    and soon, soon

the bones shall be wrapped in yesterday's news.

and the incinerator burns crayon yellow
        as the trains slink along the sunset
past the piles of cut grass,
past the rooster-moulded trees,
past mauve butterflies on white weather-board,
past concrete girls on topless patios
aged with waiting for blooms and perfect rainfalls
with leafless bodies gliding through the fern-sea,

thinking of growing forever

UNNAMED VII

In a state of limitless time we move along
Bathing ourselves in the sleek foam of the ocean
Gliding in crests, and the water stinging the eyes
Choking when we drink it, gently lulling us back
To shore. Then the sand strikes us, reddening
Our skins, sticking in the hair, and our nostrils
Yet giving sensations.
Slowly we dress our bodies with towels, or
Stretch ourselves on the white sand and close our eyes.
No thing in the sky but the sun: which is hot
In the summer, and hangs on the top of the blue
While we feel this warmth, and wish
The wind did not blow, for the sand will stick again
To the face.

Z
A N
Y

WHITE TELEPHONE

The white telephone, stark,
in unsilent dark
the mushroom darkness
expanding
like the universe

the white telephone, erupting
in the ancient night
making demands
that I cannot accept
in the sullen haze of sleep
please
make me unknown
for awhile
make my telephone
       black
in the dank fakeness
of the midnight
       suburban
calm

EARWIG

Earwigs used to bother me
kindly, kindly, don't touch me
keep your distance
from my thick ear
I don't want another fear
to walk after me when other
                              shameful
shades have sunk back
                    into
dark, dark places:

but now I've lit a light
inside the tubes inside my head,
and I let earwigs scuttle bravely in and out,

there isn't a neuron that isn't a site
for the havoc and the banquets
of that introspective and curious
                              feral
being that is so fond
of the devious and transparent
behemothian corridors of the
                              cogito ergo sum
of my unlucky mind.

Lovers

THAMMUZ WITH ASTARTE: 2000

I am lorn and filled with rain
from spring winter sky
I see the crystal man and girl
in amber lie

through the telephone I cry
anonymously
in the night
where my car has been parked
in the while
spirit light of maytime moon
I am lorn
in the red steel place
where voices lie

where voices lie

and the tinfoil flitter of rain
in the hollow no exit of the street
where I crouch in the fleet
transience of the booth where I am filled
                              with night pain

the coinage of the realm slip through
my eyes rain drenched and dreaming
stare hard through cinematic light
at the instructions for calls

at the instructions for calls

I am calling anonymously in the might or
right of the winter that has come in spring.

I spent two hours erect by the car in the rain
before I to this pillar of voices did come
before I to this dark tower came.

when you respond from seven thousand miles away
I say;
Elaine, Elaine, I am lorn
for you
the rain is coming down all round
my head

Elaine said:

The telephone wire is garland
around our necks.

and we hung on
        regardless
of cost
        uttering
the cheap expenditure of the words
because on a telephone
it's foolishness to despise them
and the telephone operators from

Mexico to here gave us amber time

for the crystal man
for the crystal lady

as they spoke what pages may,
without much deletion
leave unspoken
        forever and ever

I walked out of the acrid
        communication center
        my heart
        was
        on

W   I   N   G   S

        and
        my
        blood
        said

    S   I   N   G

and I walked home
        in the
lilt of the rain
leaving my car parked
        in the white light
    all night

NEARLY LOSING LUCY

Lucy was gone, pedaling down the beach on her
naked feet
to the sharp oyster-beds
my heart was a gong beating with fear
as I went after her in thick boots.

I found Lucy watching the anemones
in a pool, warm in the mid-day
she smiled trucefully at me

the oysters had slashed her feet
and the sea-lice, like time, had begun to feed
feeding on Lucy's feet
while she offered her big toe like a nipple
to the lips of an anemone

if Sam Peckinpah had made the scene
or David Lean, the audience could not have seen
more pathos.

I knelt beside her while the sirens of the sea
played in my pleading brain
I ran my fingers through her strands of hair, the
magical lyre
that charmed the singers of the choir
inside my shaking head.

I took an orange from my bag
and peeled it, squatting on the rocks,
Lucy beside me like a rag
from heaven drenched with tears
and blood and sprayed with the waters
from the oceans

Seven segments of hot Mediterranean orange I laid
between her legs on the oyster-bed,
my propitiation for something I'd said.
She threw the segments one by one into the pool
while I battered the innocent shellfish with a
heavy stone
the angry worshipper whose sacrifice has been
sent home.

I ran my fingers through her lyre of hair again
the magical lyre that made my head sing with pain.

She bent down then, and snatched a sea-egg from
the pool
its hedgehog prickles waving in alarm
so she cupped it in her hands, her body hunched
over as she squeezed the kina, crushed it hard
until the needling sensors must have made her bleed

then she stood upright in the pool
and threw the sea-egg to the waves
as I stared like a portrait of the village fool
at orange pieces floating round her knees,

until I took the truth for what it was
and began to use my tongue
to say what I had hoped the sweet segments
of the orange would have said,
that this cute appeal, sweet and young,
in its mute consummation would have saved

the exposure of my proud voice.

Our arms reached out through the rainbows
between us
the rainbows made by the sun and the spray
we kissed in the water, she smiled and I choked
and we stood

Lucy let me carry her,
for her feet still bled
I carried her over the oyster bed
my steel-shod boots crunching on the shells harsh
and sharp,
as I carried her like a holy grail
with her lips warm on my cheek.

PICKING UP YOUR SCENT

I sense you now
your stale ice perfume
on your sharp sweat
the perfume that guaranteed
you immune from the marches
of mortal decay –
           well not from decay,
but from the body wastes,
its unwanted liquids on the skin,
so when I browse over
your shoulder
the rankness is like
rotten peaches
in the fridge

even when you placed
a bunch of violets
on the dresser,

your breath mixes with mine
its tired digested old port wine
huffing on me like a wolf
on the doors of the three pigs.

Your taste is a long overstayer
in my mouth

I go to my fridge
to find the cherries,
not quite thawed
that I will use to whisk
away the fur that you have left

but they are gone.

I remember now
you said before you left
you wanted something cold
to chase it down and leave you
feeling fresh.

BANGLADESH!
was the worst
that I could think of
as I stood on
the cold lino at 6 a.m.
light flooding the wretched kitchen from the fridge

that I had hoped
would save me
from remembering you.

I in the sky saw a seagull float
it was a Chinese kite
my brain saw that
to give me pain

because the seagull had this disability,
it could not be retained forever.

she was my bird, she was my kite,
and,
even knowing how it had to be a trap
she was on her knees and my head was in her lap

well I made the mistake
of casting my eye to the broad sky
you'll die it said dying is near

there's no way left? I said
thinking that Bergman can't have scripted death
into all things
and thinking also
of Chicken-licken

we were on the grass by the sea
and we had come sauntering

along the path made of cool clay.

I know she came and loved me then

but the sky revealed to me that I was dying
I found out then too
how hell can turn from red to blue.

LADY OF UNSUDDEN DECISIONS

You don't believe me lady of unsudden
decisions
when I say,
in the envy of ecstasy,
I passionately
claim my daemonic desira
your love

never quintuplex
O madonic madam,
       for,
in the tor est noir fortuitime,
I wanted so much
       to call you heather
in the springtime lost mirror seven years
broken

O give me, offer me your hand,
token it in alabaster
memories

I didn't know.
what you shouted at me from
the other side of the street.

I followed palm ordained arcanic
rite
across your hand
and I see so pertinently the swing
of your soft eyes gray,
the porous lightscreen,
a projection
        where costumes rustle
in the islets
        yes islets
of your common courtesy

let
the opal
rest.

carried her arching in water.
In my arms.
forming.
unable to tell, yet.
back to the water, charioteering. Cheering.
                              in my arms.
crowning glory rampant.
by the banks.
    EXULTATE
overt exhalations frisking my mouth.
the orifices like
pooled anemones.
blow over the hill, you.
need not.
    JUBILATE
there we were happy

by the stream at the klondike valley
of goldbride blushes
icewater on the gonads. jumpshrink.
falls swimming in a ton of tides.
    betide.
the wooing of. the learner.

burn her.
out.
dried in summer. leaves. untended in.

the mountains unspied. the tower.
watched wither waves of flame.

dement her.

do you recall that
day.
upstream.
spreadeagered joy.
decloy thy words.

parried her. parching in water. in my arms.
chary of chariots
daisybrains and muttercups.

blow.

spent dementia.
in the thyme'n browning blossom bush at 3 o'clock.

oh.
come hewing from the water in.
maytime ice. blew my balls not my mind.
your blue bit-tits.

linking your knees. breeze from the scent of.
maddened drowning glory flower.

we were. there.
once.

Published in ARGOT, December 1972   

LITERARY
Journeys

LITERARY JOURNEYS IN DORCHESTER

Near the Weymouth pier,
where a fortune-teller named Zara read my stars,
We met a tiny woman standing on the strand
yes, taller than knee-high to a grasshopper,
but only as far as your elbow, lower with taller folks,
and we got chatting, she and us,
waiting in line for the Dorchester bus,
she was diminutive but she had largesse,
made us feel part of the whole scheme of things,
hard to do in a queue,
except when you do and they do too,
spilling life stories in each other's laps,
you know they'll never be at dinner with your friends -
I'm sure she would never have had us to dinner with
her friends -
she felt charmed, though, I'm sure,
and we told her where we'd been,
to Max Gate, paying homage to the scene
where Thomas Hardy wrote the Madding Crowd,
Where Tess was born, and Jude,
where he wrote and wrote and wrote,
'Oh yes, I know of him, the goat,'
the wee wee woman said, she had him sussed,
'But he wrote like a dream,' she said, 'the old goat!' -

So you know Hardy must surely be excused,
If of Don Juan and Casanova, we do enthuse,
Should we be hard on Hardy if Eros he pursues?
You didn't know? Why, his biographers cry,
 he'd fall in love at the drop of a hat!
Tom would perform like a hot tin cat!

That's how he was, he was just doomed to adore
poetic young ladies whom he'd pore over and paw,
he was charming I'm sure,
with a peculiar ability
to wax cerebral, and act feral,
paying court to the young,
who came clad in gowns of the art nouveau
earnestly speaking of poetry's claim to flame,
it wasn't his fault if his ardour was inflamed,
not his fault Florence his last wife was thirty-nine
years younger

Still, he wrote like a dream,
Who are we, shaking our heads in 2016,
looking down the telescope of time,
who are we?
Some of us have been old goats,

and cannot even say in our defense
that at least we've written like a dream.
It's a bloody nightmare sometimes.

I remember though in his upstairs room
I found fluttering yellowly on a desk
like a newly-emerged butterfly,
a letter by hand from T.E. Lawrence,
of Arabia you know,
asking if he could one time come by,
I have a motor-cycle,
I could be there in a few minutes,
Robert Graves has recommended me
to introduce myself,
if it would not put you to unwarrantable trouble -
I stood staring out upon that garden
made for teas and scones
listening to Hardy and Lawrence converse,
they would have spoke a word or two of note.
T.E.'s own cottage was a soldier's hut.
Here where the pillars of wisdom dwelt.
Not for Lawrence mullioned windows.
Not for Lawrence a stone hewn hearth.
Not for Lawrence panelled ceilings,
Sheathed with stainless steel was his fireside,
Sheathed with tin was his upstairs room,
His adornment was mostly in his mind,
Made me think about what to leave behind.

Bringwonder (2016)   

FORGERY OF AN APPRECIATION OF JOHN KEATS BY ALEXANDER POPE

To you John Keats we give a sigh forlorn
Enabling you to scrawl to Fanny Brawn
In pathos, sickly love and cosy gaze;
Tho' let not that sigh alight on our eyes
In mewling mellow verse of printed page.
Go! Let her tell thee (if she will) to wage
Love with her: but leave the ill pen alone.
Drugged, it would seem, by some bird's petty drone
You cling to some undesignated woe
Which, splurging nothingness in place of moe
To do, persuades poor fools to ponder long
On shadows of depraved minds, which song
Suggests to them some virtue in sinking
Down to Hades when, for full count, must fling
Themselves off some high rock in ecstasy
Or merely 'cease': they for Death are thirsty
And so, being thus thirsty, so is he -
For them: which seems so beauteous they flee
Immediately through the death-channels
When I have none took and ran else.

Whyfore was this wine in th'earth imprisoned
Undrunk without cause for the unreasoned
Calculating of some grape drank craving
Fool, who hoping for the greater numbing

Of his entangled brain, he sets himself
To opening up some gloomy frozen gulf
In vain toil-sweatened by the swinging spike
Where after some long night's wearisome hike
Down to the holed innards of the earth
Laden with choicest wine he makes worth
His labours in reverently placing
(with fix-starred eyes on the manna gazing)
In the deep bowels casks of vintage pure
Then rests it there for ages to endure
So, when the barrels ache and almost split
And he is wizened with his empty wit
He throughs open the sunk vaults and washes
His gullet with liquor, while joshes
Bacchus and his compatriots, to see
A white-haired dodderer sprawl in a sea
Of wine, and thanking Flora while gurgling
His fancies of the rustic dance ogling
At the gaseous movement at the brim
Of his uncouth tankard, letting reason
Die, Perchance he will some other folly
pursue; pour nostalgic tears o'er holly
That ne'er decked the halls of medieval age
Save in the visions boundless of the sage,
John Keats, who leaps through chasms never leapt
And sees by Chronos how stone castle slept
In darkened ages, all flown now to giant
Glass-stained cathedrals, where air is rampant
With the heavy stench of Middle Years.

So he cleans the blood from all the windows
Replaces stodgy flavoured flour by red
And beauteous jellies, makes the bed
Seem soft and flowing for sleep's passage
So he takes a true picture, its visage
He paints some colour,
where before there was little else than a funereal pose.

Thus let us bid him a lofty farewell
And hope to grace our minds with thoughts that tell.

EDMUND SPENSER'S DREAM

It was the young girl sitting in the old man
Leeching cruelly for his blood
They meandered by a glossy stream
Where often lilies taught the light
How to behave

Most cruelly has she sought his blood
At a circus fair entertaining him
For all his worth on the monkey's cage
Then in a pasture act the dud
Then in a bare church out on a limb
Play Congregations with a burnt page.

At the tower at the high window at dawn
She leeched blood from all his taps
Weary taps
Yet still must knock his parchment brawn
In manacles bright (soft by the hard bone)

There I saw him stripped and stretched
In that tall chink at daybreak
At his spine I heard a bird peck
And as he screamed I held the bowl
Well in the groin, deep in the well
As a gentle hind on the tiger, fed:
Yet shortly: for as it flutters bleeding
She has made it refuse.

A *Higher* PLACE

ULTIMACY
(completed 20th July 1963)

O thou moon!
Jolted through the heav'ns through the no-ness
Glimm'ring down the rained skies
Drawing thine silver cords taught
Nearer thus me, and all thine all: all his captives
Wrangling strings from mundane brain - down-
to-earth thoughts
Tying them in a lute, to charm the still unslain
Grasping with the craving strength of lunar force
Casting o'er the curved light-bound
Hand, which, placing bounds must wave a million
Like it in its sight: and holding while it does
Endless alphas, infinite omegas.
Swirling the hand's blood, sucked from the veins,
The great curves fling it to the blue-grey hills
And so to course through me.

Ray the paths through me
Let attraction, attract, with force akin to thee
Drown my static with your undiluted
Race me for embrace with the whole
Fondle the warm, slide the hand across the skin
Blinding screen of pierced light unconceived
Clashing the black clouds shimm'ring o'er
The blank souls.

Wisping the dry grass rhythmic o'er the wet fields:
Sun burns, and so the ground is dry: and so the welts
Have sapped the strength. Thus is the light
So cold, yet scorching beyond senses
Or percussion. Left only the glistening bones
That hung once beauty sensual choking
Breath in the roaring of the blood-beat
Racing this body-fluid to embrace the accessible eros
While there to know the flesh; and heat
Exuding ruddy, scalding each pore in passing forth.
In flowing folds hung that beauty
On the white framework
Firm the petal cloth encompassing, soft
For hands to admire, there to be and be.
Save that now the air is clothes to standing hangers.

Ah! No longer shall the taunting sneers dash the face
Catch the breath, knock away balance, kill strife
For they scream through beams invisible to natural sight
Sight blinded by lunar flung to palm of hand.
More the flushing of shining silver glazed
To absorb the image, glow it in the palm
Kindle, and set to arc through the cosmos
Placed centre of the two roads, sapping eternal force
'Till centre vanishes as the rods, and the gassed sparks

Yet that was conscious: so the knowing
Is caught at the end in the force-stream
Becoming such the medium
Then let the knife tear the fleshly heart,
The earth gape, and pour their transcendence
Into the greatness of the hillness and the song:
Chasms close, th' blue mountains become plains
The hand clasp itself about earth's crystal orb
That satellites above, amongst the stars
Conversing with the Heav'ns. No longer
Shall it reflect sun's divine rays, nor run blood:
No longer is it there, but immortal pattern
Of energy, force into predestined state.

So the hand wrings jubilant with others, numbering
Numberless. So it sets the spark to Adam's greenery
Freeing and releasing the form of the atom
Disbanding electricity, all mass, all shape
Letting me curve through the spiral, splintering
The last curl, being absorbed 'mongst the gone
Captives of the moon: all enfolding about me,
And me them, to entreat and be answered;
While towering the centre of the hands
Centre where the tinglings loved through space
Centre, towering and powerful alpha of omega
Shudders me, pronounce to resonate
Waves and waves of shockened thought
Breaking and tearing upon accumulative known
Making it apart, and set from resemblance

Of any structure.
So myself is the centre, and lunar captives
Have ringed themselves about
Finally flinging from the farthest hand but millions
The onslaught, torment and absorption
Tying entirety to all eternity.

UNNAMED IV

O God!
Let us see You, let us see Your creation
Let us see Your fields, waters, the very skies
Let us live through time
And live by You

O God!
That gave us to ourselves
Our mad ways, our invincible spirit
Humour to be human, and flesh
To know You.

O God!
How tolerant, merciful, and fall of humour
For our actions; how conscious
Of our shortcomings, and of we
Who make the shortcomings.
O God!
While some can prate with intellectual gait
I say only You love.

THE
HUMAN
CONDITION

HOW WELL DO YOU HOLD
UP TO WEAR AND TEAR?

If you hold people up to the light
their first thought is about their opacity
but stretch them a little, make the light bright
don't be ashamed of audacity

if you are through the water-marks show
silhouette puppets in a theater of shadow
adjust the light source, the mark will soon glow:
for some the worms from cave will do
for others, none other than Hiroshimas

Here is the circuit controlling the tear-dust
makes them cry hard, they need a cathartic
they'll probably squirm and say it's your turn
but catharsis is not all that you want them to learn.

This one is old and unused to the light
scribbled and drawn on, used as a wrapper
she's had hard times, but she has no right
to immolate herself.

Some people go like parchment, others like vellum
others go like newsprint or facial tissues
it's no wonder light fall through the fissures
bypassing the Paper College's Stamp of Perfection

so that some cats are only useful rolled out flat
covered up in imprints, misprints and graphics
or song like FRAGILE and THIS END UP and
FINGER LICKIN' GOOD –
and in the end they only get ripped off.

INSIDE YOURSELF: THE WORDING OF BACON'S PAINTINGS

How are you inside yourself?
The skin that invites a hold on your kidney guests
will it divide at the offal-mongerer's request?

sudden and fell, delighted death
slips in his nib and draws you up
   (knees to chest the feet they kick)
slides into your well
that tried not to betray
a ripple
of dissent
yet bravely you breast the waves,
your spleen displaced
your milk run dry

Do you think you'll bear up?
the ductless glands and the liverpools
in the twitching hour of night may overturn
      by underhand
methods quite over your head
without consultation
your skin
may
divide
lots

over your seal-broken state
and no promise will be binding –

and all those coin-droppings by the wistful wells
          of memorial parks
are only wage-pools for tomb-robbers
who unlock us if we look pale
and ransack our drawers
diving into our hallowed moth-killing wardrobes,
                    and the one who nicks
        the jewels
cops the lot.

Your relatives ask for an inquest.
The coroner is dumbfounded when they sound
him out
at the pathologist's report
which will probably be
suppressed.

STRANGE WOMAN

and I met you only a moment past,
so strange you are,
          strange woman
yet I know you intimately,
your heavy bone face in bas-relief stares down
and my heart burns with ecstasy
to know that you are who I thought
that ghoul with curlers in her hair
putting out the tea-cups on formica
rattling the crimson brittle nails
                    in
preparation for the witch ladies
who stir sugar into their table-topics
laden with dangerous sex anecdotes
yes why not lace the tea with sherry,
and ungirdle the crimpolene dress and remove the pearls,
I am so intimate with you, ghoul lady,
bone of bone, flesh of flesh,

rattling formica
against the emigration of the lonely thoughts

and you do haunt me,
          in the streets
you taunt your children and pan their brains
why do you not scan your innard thinkings

with Jackie Kennedy and pimples on your mind
you hardly dare
and your flesh suffocates me,
in the goat which travels through the snow
you still follow me,
breathing,
    breathing
your shallow mist into my ears,
the amplified shellseasound
                              of
astronauts recorded while they sleep
before they perish

your laugh it fears me, chases me
far into the catacombs where I meet
        poor old
    Demosthenes
stammering his way through an address to the plebeians

and finally you refuse to weep, you
                          scarf
up your head in harsh shrouds,
                          bold fronting
all your sorrow
        and
despising your little child who cries at night

and you so strange woman
                    you
never pursue the footsteps of the night
                              you
bring them on,
you whisper, come closer, closer
bring nightmares into the squid dark wake
fullness

I do not want you, ghoul woman, slopping at me
                         like at a tide
or sentient fungoid suckers on a field of battle,
however it is,
I do not want you,
          with your
slug wastes swelling your tight skin
and your thick abused lips
which when they part reveal a skeleton and not a smile
and I am so ecstatic, for
I have met you before,
          in so many boutiques
and even in the lovely lilting forests of the spring,

I know how to flee from you,
                    and I do
before your scalp sprouts serpents
you are so strange, strange woman
and you are everywhere

A GRETA GARBO THING

If I spoke not a word from my birth
                              to my death
from the birth of my death and the death
of my birth

no one would mind
                    or find
cause to consider it strange
                    or deranged
since the privacy is a respectable cause
a way for the solitary to behave
introspectively
it saves
explanations
to be known
as someone who prefers
to be alone

I can lay down in a shell,
                    irrespective
of the search parties who've been
                              sent out
to bring me back dead or alive
while I abound
in the infinite space of my shell,

and huge faces come to look at me in a shell
they come to see me naked in a shell
as when I woke in the corral
of infancy
in the deep wildness of the dusk
in the fierce deep of the husked hood
of childworld
when I at the wake
                of my tumbling sleep
saw vast heads nodding
over my face
looking cold and confident, fresh
from carnivals and processions

wanting me
the heads were wanting me
to beach my shell
to reach out for the bright vision
of extraversion.

But the search for those who lie in shells
isn't protracted.

The supersonic whistles soon
gather dust

and no one comes to loom
cheerfully communicado

waiting to drop
pebbles in the pond

soon
there is no disturbance
                on the surface
all the pens have been put away,
and radios and telephones are reduced
to their components

no opponent
        speakers come to hail
                the silent figure
because privacy is a respectable cause
it saves so many

explanations

EXILES

If what has happened were unspeakable,
Who can we find to speak to?
Who will open mouth to utter word -
Breath better saved for comforting a child.
Where then were you going to divert the flood
When they came asking you about your sister
and your father
Did you think you could stop your tears
Just because a billion people watched?
The last I saw, our house was burning
We sat down in the hot fire by a tree
And a leaf fell off.
My child put the leaf into his pocket.
Where're your leaves going to blow to,
After we have flavoured you with the smoke
From our fires?
Who can read the inscriptions on burned
leaves anyway?
Whose faces will you smoke-scarred ones see
across flaming ash heaps
before you too are consumed?

THE TRAVELLER

THE MOVING LOTUS

satraps from Siam on elephants
mauve jewels in their mouths
Kipling poems in their pocketbooks

O Victoria
where are you now

to turn to knowledge
we must conceive Rutherford atoms
and electron clouds of diamond dust
jesus show some pity
Jupiter must be galling in its size
on a bicycle ride through space
I never met the girl that I intended
passing sugar-lumps into the threatening teeth
of the harmless steed

O druids
of past rituals
say an epic to us now

we effervesce but never rise
and anguish clouds
ascend irrationally to Mercury
where transmutations fructify

O girl with amethysts
dewy cobwebs in your hair
fresh flower in all your hollows
ethereal girl
move closer to the scent of Piccadilly Circus
where they swung from the Atlantean chandeliers
erected by the waterels of '23
there we shall adore life (and death, too)

IN THE GRIP OF THE WHEEL

I at the gas-station with the greek friend
in the cold sausage hours of 3 a.m.
fighting through icy cans for rags
to test the oil

the slot machines for super doesn't work
and the standard does.
We stroke the engine sadly, lighting fags
it won't like the standard fuel

but it gets it on, and pinking melancholically
thrusts past the molecules of cosmos
we smile and open a pack of cadbury's toffee
that looks too much like plastic explosive
to make sense
            to sensitive
people.
We
beam exclusively into the streets
drifting past
            like mechanical studioscapes
we the beautiful people are better than they,
they who lie asleep in middle-class cocoons
hoping that breakfast will never come –

how far have we included in our visions
the ones we abhor?

We pass a joint around and call each other cool
we call the others straight,
speaking of a culture shock
a future shock.

We welcome one another to our nightmares,
choosing 2 a.m. to begin our travels
inside the petty capsule of the car.

It is a place of metamorphosis
detached, in mobile stasis
we're ten billion galaxies
away
looking at earth
through a radio telescope
we're dedicated to blind prophecy

I grip the wheel at 4 o'clock
while my friend grinning begins to mock
a Lebanese poet of no antiquity.

The wheel is in my grip,
but the engine hates the standard fuel.

A girl in black stumbles beneath the sodium light
she walks like a butterfly without its wings.
We stop and Petros steps out
(you've got to do this on the road)

the girl leans on the lamp-post
opens her coat.
Mists rise from her mouth.
She opens a pack and finds it empty
crushes it and throws it at our car.
Her coat parts and she is naked.

I think leaning on the wheel:
This is a fantasy.

Petros talks to her without words,
doing his best.
she gives him the scornful finger,
reaches out and feels autistically
between his legs
then walks to a house.
She takes the plug out
light splashes
into our detached stasis
into our space.

her head twists right round to us
but like a wooden toy snaps back into place.

She passes through the plug hole.
light and sounds are leaking out
the sound of GENESIS. of heavy rock.
Pictures too
tumble through
this leak into another universe.
A silhouetted boy stands in space

arm encircled around his waist
and pisses in his leisured haste
onto the path.

The door shut.
The hole is plugged.
The light can only hiss
through cracks,
spilling
unwanted
into places
that pay back nothing.

Petros and I move on.
The engine has overheated in the meantime
but we are prepared
and outside the Tao Yueh restaurant
we turn our travel capsule into a steaming dragon
which persists ferociously.
We fill the radiator with new water
We depart for Hamilton.

I wonder how much compassion
we have left to us
after the passion
of fulfillment.

The radio plays with an interview with the third world
we're just waiting, they say
we're just awaiting the awakening of the world.

we smile in empathy
from the rarefield, loving and Himalayan
heights.

The road is a roaring triangle in perspective.
We drive for the apex.
We smoke
port royal
listening to the all-night show
stuck, as the singer says,
inside a mobile.

Our moving capsule travels
through the sick gut of the land
that down the dark line of duty
wallows all
the pretty capsules
that travel through
its night,
yet there's no cure
without attachment.

for we'll travel on and off the Desert Road
until the world runs out of oil
and we run out of gold,
feeling the question that Ulysses made old,
If staying power does not belong to the voyager,
what is the name of the power
that does belong?

WITH A

TwINKLE

IN HIS
EYE

THE GREAT
EVENSONG SCANDAL

In the cathedral the heads are all singing
counting the tolls of the gone and the living
with gongs at the altar and minds of unchange
where nothing can alter the counting of change

the green cloth souses the coin-clink.
instead, like a roof-patter of rain, or drips on leaves,
the metal money taps the paper money and I think
of dry dirt knocking on a coffin like thieves

(the mourners usually do steal the moment)

the servers move the lever of the louvres
– it's hellish hot – discreetly, and roses
 lasciviously flop through the chinks in manoeuvres
 of petal and thorn and bushes on fire just for Moses.

Everyone is very Solomon.

A lust of wind hustles in a pus of petals
That creep, as bold as fingers from the marsh decaying,
down the sere severity of old ladies' necks.

The aged Boer veteran in himself a chronicle

of campaigns is mostly a chronical hiccupper.
He sits alone: he is garlic sodden and fickle.
His hiccups sound like God impetuously declaring
Armageddon
with verberating dry retches
that drown the trumpet blasts
and turn even coroners green:

yet we sit in wonder and strain to hear him smother
for the soldier is an artist
and no one retch can be heard without the other
and each dry retch competes for escape
like hell's stinking thunder
Too long kept down by angels

until in spiralling nightmare the exorcised
protesting demon exits
like a cosmic train, shrieking and belching
from umpteen black and clockless space

into the pierced elegance of pearly ears.

Evensong for more than twenty-one years
Has been a congregational constitutional
Of a fortitude amounting to an intestinal institution.

No visitor has ever failed to be impressed.

Tonight the veteran, during a mild imitation
of a dyspeptic ulcer-ridden vacuum-cleaner
sucks in a swoop of petals that would have
clogged the bogs of Europe for a week.

He regurgitates them sullenly, discreetly.
The survivor of the Boer War regards each petal
As a kind of ballistic triumph:
This hour the boor is in his finest fettle.

The king priest furls his face into a crunched walnut,
passes the fetters of love to the curate,
and liberated, turns into a convolvulus of hatred,
and wrathing at the mouth, with no sound commands
that this botanical intrusion into divine service,
these tares amongst the wheat,
be cast out and at a latter time
sprayed into submission.

The Chief Server wrestles with the louvre-lever
He treats it like the groaning winches of a mighty
draw-bridge
Ancient and fell, mounted against attack from knight
and churl.
Preoccupied, he tips the coin and note
into the bosom of the local good-time girl.

The suppressed giggles spread like a silent and ill-
timed fart
which, bottled up for too long, comes as a sudden
forgotten enemy
making hydrogen disulphide in comparison like
lavender.
A Windsor-looking equestrian lady, to her
neighbour
whispers (in the old, melodramatic manner)
"That girl's the devil's own daughter."
(The Windsor-looking equestrian lady
is a fan of Dennis Wheatly, the writer of
foul, black and thoroughly magical writes:
To her, every trollop in a church
Is secretly a tart in Satan's kitchen – "By rights
A type like her should be flogged with birch.")

RETRIEVING THE COLLECTION

In the vestry office, Satan's tart peels off her crust
Her friends, in sundry places split with laughter,
Assist as Salome throws off her seven veils
"No bra, Sally?" "That's right, she's braless,
One of the liberated generation."
"Then where's the cash?'

"You mean the money from the plate?
It's collected inside my nylon panties

Though I'll never know how it got past the elastic."

No attempt is made any more to be staid.
But the congregation collectively assumes the morality
of the stiffest, tightest laced virginal old maid,
It is affronted and knock-kneed, bedeviled, racked and petrified
By hysterical hoots of a loose unmuzzled laughter
Wanton laughter, unbridled, unleashed,
unshackled, unthrifty and unlicensed:

And grimly spoke the vestryman, I'll see to her.
He turns the handle
"Wretched slut
You're a filthy disgrace.
MY GOD SHE'S UNLACED!
SHE'S STARKERS! SHE'S __"
"Keep your voice down Sam"
says an older man.

Sally with hands very piously cupped
Holds the filthy lucre up
"Here it is" (she can't help grinning)
"It slipped into my nylon briefs
Nearly made me come to grief.
Well it's not my fault __ I didn't put it there, silly."

Sam in the ruins clutches at straws –
The only ones there are the coins and the notes
which he holds high and tight in his fists like a
prophet
As, appropriate to all visions,
The blinding light of revelation comes:
a photographic flash from the local news,

capturing forever the naked girl still grinning
surrounded by vestrymen clutching fistfuls of
ready money

whilst in the midst of the congregation
there are various and pleasant conversaziones
of unnatural acts, libidinous blasphemies
libels, homicide and moral conflagration.

Later the Red Cross is called to halt an invasion
of an apoplectic epidemical prostration.

The old warrior of the Boer Wars is unperturbed.
He is an inveterate veteran of many campaigns.
"Not as good as the girls and the nightspots in
Capetown,"
he muses,
"but livening up."

MR POTATO MAN

The draughtsman plays artistry
On paper
Like a child with Mr Potato Man
Sticking on the head
Adding the ears
And the funny nose,
Dangling dark spectacles
Over the eyes
So that the cries
Can be more or less
Stifled:
(Old wives say
Eyes
Are the portals of the soul
Which accounts for the dark glasses
Being so fashionable)

by the doneover stall at the station
the boys approach the flower-lady who
reads the letters from her aunt
interspersed
between the pages of cantgraphic rites
of multiple relationships

the boys jell tantalized
                as
the Minister spends eight dollars on a magazine
prepared preferentially for psychology students

boys that will be fifteen cents violets
are always nice to get the stay
                        fresh
as a Martian maiden's matrix
in the place where goats stroll between
the legs of horses twenty hands high and green:

we look over the counter, mother, and we see
extending far the shining covers which seem
all to contain
        hints
of pubic hair and public orgies

the only lilies we have today boys

are the ones with the white tongues rising
from the strong walls of wide leaves
if you would like some to take home

I am Cliff. I want to dress myself in
only glossy pages and come to your lap and sit within
the beating of your temple torch that you
                              will use
to burn me off like an African remedy for inability

I am the mother. Come to me and watch me smile
my red skin expanding under this old speckle pattern
of flowers,
and I will let you take the cellophane wrap
from the magazines and unfold the map
of all your dreams

the blinds are pulled down over the flower
and book stall
the female employee waddles to a black door
    marked:
        Ladies
on the screen of the moist white clouds
                              float
legs criss-crossed like a contortionist's prescription
for perfumed ecstasy

and when the white clouds leave

they the males are naked under the twilight
sodium-lit station network

waiting
for the great woman to emerge from the black door
lilies in her basket

Published in ARGOT, August 1972

QUANTUM

Last night on the sofa my wife turned and asked
What's quantum? What's quantum? Yes quantum!
I wanted to get to the bottom,
So I tried to think very fast -
What's quantum, I said to my kind,
Spit it out! Don't delay!
But all that came out was a laugh,
My wife only does simple stuff
anything else would be far too tough -
It was ten p.m. and here I was tasked
With defining what the dickens is quantum,
I was momentarily struck paralytically dumb
A condition with which I'm not typically lumbered
Now I'm sure you're familiar with that word APLOMB?
I can usually summon oodles of aplomb
But when confronted with quantum
That space-time conundrum
My brain ballooned into a mischievous water Bomb
Ready to burst showering drops on a playground.
Words wouldn't come, so I only laughed,
I remembered Benjamin Button
I recalled Brownian Movement and dear
Dr Who
My mind feverishly invoked interstellar
I saw particles dancing the jitterbug
I nervously scanned stroboscopic electrons

Barely perceptibly bouncing with photons energies
charging with random
abandon flirting through galaxies carted on a golf ball
with President Donald
Trump in control, the universe we knew and loved so
well going
unaccountably AWOL lost in the zero of God's black
hole anything a possible,
its quantum!
But my wife's head was shaking her eyes they did roll,
It didn't help when I rabbits on about Max Planck in
nineteen hundred and
two
Or corroborating papers by Einstein
In nineteen hundred and five -
She told me that frankly my dear
She didn't give a damn
About Heisenberg's improbable principle
She just wanted me to sing something simple,
She just wanted to instantly know
How does mentioning quantum quite fit
into this book where really it talks
Most of the time about miracles -
Isn't it rather weirdly mysteries
to link up the word quantum to miracle?
Just answer me quick!

Don't ramble! What a pillock!
I want to get on with my miracle book!
Then an epiphany took hold as I shook
with the frenzy of laughter hysterical,
Quantum is easy,
who needs all that theory,
even a chicken can tell you!
The answer lies in Trump's balls,
In his golf balls I mean,
for its true, the centre can't hold,
things will fall apart, threads will be unravelled
amongst the rubbery stuff of space so curvaceous,
It's really quite lyrical!
Quantum is a miracle!
That's what the book is about!
I've only got to the middle, I know,
But I'll have to stop here
It's getting beyond me
For the question was posed very late in the hour,
so farewell my quantum,
We've not got to the bottoms
It's a tack and messy hysterical mystery,
Aluminous miracle spinning in space,
(Oh I do hope you have left some oysters for me,
for the walrus is
unconsciously greedy.)

KITH
AND
Kin

HIKING THROUGH THE SCRUB TO UNCLE THICK

gorse-flower on your knees, recall
the itchy heat?

in a hotel lobby, come on uncle!

what comes of the second stage?
burning off the flower, the first.

your bushambled disgraceful pants – go on, page:0
(the electric clock hums, clicks its teeth, he's late.)

the second stage when the flower flames down
and away
umbrellas forth the green enamel claw
carding the denim into cotton waste
scrumming over the coast, with ti-tree there, and
horse flies:
during the resistance, your thighs bleeding, you
were thirsty

in uncle's hotel
from lobby to bar the vertical mirrors imaged
the omissions of polished wood

sunstroke was branding Sydney

when you emerged
changed out of your tarnished slacks
and your tarlatan blouse
and keen, you slipped into a rock-pool
mothering the anemones

The trained voice pages through the system:
Paging Mister Thick, paging Mister Thick

Drowsing in the amniotic pool
you the lizard watched, coming from the sea
the skin-diver with the spear
who beside you, hushing, peeled off her gear
Uncle smiles spikily, sound as basinware
bristling and sharp as coir
bringing up drinks and a chair
digging in.

IT'S YOUR MOTHER
AT THE DOOR

rain draggled, mud drying around the hem
of her speckled ermine gaberdeen

standing up, waiting
treating herself to a waffle
the cylinder biscuit quaking open
real cream seeping through
like blood through the cracked pavements
of the intricate lips,

the tampered doors
where few have passed

that held open the straits
for ages
before barring the shaggy ships

rain scraggled,
            her mind beside the wringer pours
into the durable clinch of her hands
which when the waffle is gone
take up again the perpetual motion
of snakes and vines.

The rain has fallen on her spectacles.
she lifts her head:

a fifty-cent one-minute sketch,
the sideshow sketchman,
trying to be instant,
              busily
moves his coloured pencils
over the cartridge paper

putting in the lines and shades

the lines and shades

she'd wanted always for a likeness to be found
not to do her like Pietri Anagoni
or a da Vinci
only
the ancient aching for a likeness –
a revelation of her business
here

she did not long for passing commentaries –
"He's got your mouth just right"
that holds the anguish of her years,
withheld
in its tight compression
the inward sips of sorrow sculptured
like a signpost in the flesh

she sits on the chair that folds up again
on a platform elevated
on a closed television circuit
for the five thousand pairs of eyes
that wish to behold
the making of a portraiture

she smiles a little,
so the sketchman does,
takes her coat
sets up his paper
and his affinity

a sixty-second laser link

that mystifies, appalls the crowd
who grows
quiet
like desert blooms at daybreak

their mystic consciousness
expanded
otherwise why say the crowd
grows silent?

the fruit of the golden silence hangs
on the tree of transcendence
before substance

the golden fruit hangs
on the slumbering and intricate
knowledge

The conversational rhubarb begins to speak.
It is finished.
From the closed circuit released
                             she
stumbles from the chair
                   where
the artist holds her coat
and her elbow
as she makes her way
step by step down,
the likeness in her basket,
thinking of undone housework.

The picture on the sideboard shows
the ears and cheeks and hair,
                         clearly
neutral, and the eyes thus passionately blanks
like the eyes of her doll when they would look
no more
and the cheek into a dark vale fallen
is the furthest he would take
his pencils on that crooked journey
through the face

the mouth parts
a wiry knowing crinkle
in the tree

and she departs
to make the tea.

BLESSING (FOR A WEDDING)

May the love that now blossoms from
Your heart and soul,
May it ignite the fuse that through the
green force drives the flower,
may these flowers of love
ever unfold from the buds of your hearts,
may you love your man
may you love your woman
with might and main,
and may you morning awakenings be peaceful and
sweet,
may you arise from your bed
filled with joy
may the creative breath flow through
your souls,
woven together in the loom of your
love,
and may your children be inspired
by the threads of love's power
to find their own gifts.
May the remembrance of rapture
carry you on the rough surf of life's ocean.
May you ride on the joy of this day.

UNTITLED

With ink-stained fingers ken these words,
the slow unsteadiness tea-drinking beside the
woods
with my daughter on the green couch writing
poems
We so close to beloved bush, it seems
there is no separation,
thin glass fails to cut us off
from the wood-pigeon at play diving in the air
the fantails dancing in the king ferns fronds
the kingfisher
strongly speaking from the power-lines
The tuis climbing in the flax, exquisitely,
drinking nectar -
We wander into the porch where the wet cat sits
and the soft rain that has fallen all night
now falls in us,
like the first tender coming
of waters
dripping from the skies of new planets
Into bud-bursting earth that has long desired
a rain.

Jan 13 1999

SESTINA IMPERFECT

Standing with his father by the cooling stone
In the wind and conscious of complete
Unprivacy before the columns of colouring lights,
Aware of numbers of hurrying people,
He begins to listen to notes playing within
His own, mutely on a piano, covering a very little range

A simple friendly scale, that softly and not alone
Speaks of five or six in a still warm room replete
With his own father conversing of well-liked nights
Sharing concentration (such as looking at a well-built
steeple)
Even as the day wears on their clothes grow thin
The father makes an ugly face to tempt the wind to change.

The notes expired on an old brown tone
The boy looks up and hears the fingers of his father beat
One against the other in casual cracking flights
Of fancy as he talks to table of smiling tender people
The child standing on the pavement who knows no sin
Feels the cool graying evening in streets too strange.

Still the father stands with his hands concealed
Now glancing from his son to the quelling sky
Slowly wondering as today turns into yesteryear.

CABBAGES

AND

Kings

BLEMISHES

I look at the blemishes on my skin
somehow sin
looked in

the sun-yellow cheddar flakes on the lines
of my palm
as I optimistically stuff food
for the sake of nutrition, for the limbs
and the blistered skin
step in, you girls with butterflies in your burn

and toads dropping from your pert renaissance mouths
I am wondering while I lie in a phug on the grass
how golden is your skin beyond the carapace of
your jeans

how hepatitic is your blood,
and the river you've swum in,
are the fishes living
does your navel writhe like a worm
    curling   in death
or could it fit a diamond

on the sleeve which binds my sloppy organs
grow fins
and blisters flake into scales,
and there is no nutrition
just the body in a fission

RED HERRING

I admit to this day one spring bird
    A lyreing laugh
    An adult living
And one red herring.

I admit to the threshing-chamber of the day
    My unformed day
In the crux of the way
Sounded out upon a rain-reaped harvest.

I admit to this day of purple deeds
    Bright children's bangles
    Evacuees their shark-tooth necklaces
Caught up within the semblance of a herring.

16 August 1969

DREAM NO MORE

Dream no more
The dream is here.
That which you sorrowed over
As hidden in the darkness,
Twisted in the heart of the lilac,
Trammeled out of vision,
Is here before your eyes.

HAIKU

That insect breathes three hours of life –
His three-score and ten.

A girl in black stumbles beneath the sodium
                                        light
she walks like a butterfly without its wings.
We stop and Petros steps out
(you've got to do this on the road)
the girl leans on a lamp-post ~~and delights the~~
opens her coat.
Mists rise from her mouth. ~~I~~
She opens a pack and finds it empty
crushes it and throws it at our car.
Her coat parts and she is naked.

I think leaning on the wheel
This is a fantasy.
Petros talks to her without words,
doing his best. ~~~~
she gives him the ~~~~ scornful finger,
                              ,feels ~~~~ autistically
reaches ~~and~~ out and ~~gives him a double feel~~
between his legs
then walks over to a house.
She takes the plug out
light splashes ~~into our detached stasis~~
into our ~~~~ space.
Her head twists ~~~~ round ~~~~ once to us,
~~but like a wooden toy~~ snap back into place.
She passes through the plug hole.
Lights and sounds are leaking out
the sound of GENESIS. of heavy rock.
Pictures too
tumble through
~~this~~ leak into another universe.
~~A boy fills the gap.~~
A silhouetted boy stands in the space
arms encircled round his waist